A Teen's Guide to Quitting Ultra-Processed Food Now

Essential Steps to Break Free From Junk Food and Feel Your Best

C.J. Kindren

with Dr Sui H. Wong MD FRCP

© 2024 EBH Press : EBHpress.com

ISBN: 978-1-917353-57-1 (eBook), 978-1-917353-56-4 (Paperback),

978-1-917353-55-7 (Hardcover)

Table of Contents

Introduction

Are you a teen or important role model in one's life? Do you know about the effects that UPFs can have on teens?

Most of our foods go through some kind of processing. Unless you pick your own veggies and herbs from the backyard, the food you bring home from the grocery store has gone through steps, like washing or canning, to make it shelf-stable and ready to sell.

However, in our modern world, some kinds of processing that foods go through can be harmful to our health. New research is emerging on the impact that ultra-processed food (UPF) has on the human body, and the results are surprising.

One of the biggest concerns surrounding UPFs is the high amount in which they are consumed. Unfortunately, teens make up a big portion of UPF consumption, which can have a significant health impact, as teens are still developing during these formative stages. Excessive UPFs during this period in life can hinder development, thus impacting your future health.

Whether you are a teen yourself, or a parent, guardian, or teacher of one, it's essential to be informed about UPFs and how to avoid consuming them excessively. This guide will take you through the process of understanding UPFs, learning to identify them, and implementing practical strategies in your daily life to reduce their impact.

With these teen-friendly activities and exercises, you'll learn what you need to know about UPFs to change habits, find alternatives, and make choices for a long-lasting, successful future!

Chapter 1:
What's the Deal With UPF?

Ultra-processed foods are everywhere and can be especially appealing to teens, so understanding what they are will empower the next generation to make healthier decisions.

What is an ultra-processed food (UPF)? Most foods undergo changes from the farm to your table. Consider canned or frozen fruits and vegetables. These goods are processed through freezing, canning, and other methods to elongate their shelf life and make them more accessible to shoppers.

Food with excessive processing and additional additives can seriously affect our health. Examples of these foods range from potato chips, candy, and other sweets, to foods that seem healthy, like gluten-free pasta or protein bars.

In this first chapter, we will explore your health, and why it's essential to prioritize good nutrition during this pivotal time. We'll take a look at how to differentiate UPFs from other foods, as well as some of the main side effects these foods can have.

A Teen's Health

As a teen, your growing body requires nutrients to support healthy development. Long-lasting habits develop during these formative years, so setting yourself up for success is done by establishing good habits at an early age. Over time, they'll strengthen and expand, leading to more good habits.

A Teen's Growth

While your body is physically developing, good nutrition will support this growth and change. Below is a chart to help you see the major changes happening during adolescence, and what nutrition elements are needed to best support this type of growth.

What Happens During Development	Nutrition Needed to Support Growth
Brain development: During adolescence, the brain matures and forms new connections to improve brain functions. Teens can start to think more deeply than they could in childhood, allowing them to form opinions and make complex decisions. During this time, the frontal cortex continues to grow, and won't finish until your late 20s. This can result in difficulty managing impulses and mood swings (Adolescent Development, n.d.).	**Omega-3 fatty acids:** Foods rich in omega-3 help support the brain's cognitive development. Examples of foods that include omega-3 fatty acids are • fatty fish like salmon • nuts such as walnuts • seeds like flaxseed
Social changes: Throughout adolescence, teens tend to spend less time with family and more time with friends. This increase in social engagement with others can make it difficult to manage peer pressure and influence from your friend circle. This can influence behavior, emotions, and even your values.	**B-vitamins:** One study showed "higher intake of B-vitamins was protective against adolescent behavioral problems" (Allen et al, 2012). Examples of foods high in B-vitamins are • whole grains like brown rice • leafy greens such as spinach

Growth spurts:	Calcium:
After puberty, large growth spurts can result in some teens growing almost three inches a year (Reese, n.d.). This can lead to increased hunger while growing, making them more susceptible to cravings and food-related impulses.	As teens grow, calcium is essential for supporting bone development. Examples of foods high in calcium are • dairy products such as yogurt • leafy greens such as kale
Hormonal changes:	Zinc:
Changes in hormones during and after puberty can lead to many physical differences. Hormones can impact every part of your body, such as hair growth, emotions, and hunger levels.	Zinc supports immunity and reproductive hormones, a crucial mineral for adolescents. Foods high in zinc are • legumes such as lentils • nuts such as almonds

As you can see, many nutritious elements are needed to support a healthy lifestyle. The thing about ultra-processed food is that it can negatively hinder development due to:

- **Hyperpalatable foods:** This refers to foods with high sugar, fat, and carbohydrate content, which makes them taste good, but offers little to no nutrient value. Because of their high sugar or fat content, they can be very addicting, triggering cravings that may lead to overeating.

- **Changes in gut health:** Certain additives or high sugar content can disrupt your body's microbiome, a system of bacteria in your digestive system. Our gut is closely connected to our brain, so when the digestive system is disturbed, it can similarly impact the mind.

During a time of such rapid development, teens need to support their mind and body. Right now, you're studying, listening, and learning, which requires a lot of energy alone! On top of this, you're likely a part of a sport or activity that takes even more of your body's fuel. Behind the scenes, your body is growing rapidly, and all of these areas need the best support possible.

Even after knowing how important it is to provide our bodies with good nutrition, it can still be hard to break habits due to the way they've formed in our lives.

Habit Loop

Our choices impact our health. Avoiding UPFs will help ensure we provide our bodies with wholesome nutrition; however, sometimes habits can make it hard to avoid them.

Why is it that habits are so hard to avoid? There are many stages to help explain how a habit develops:

- **Cue:** First, a cue signals to your brain that it's time to participate in a routine.

- **Routine:** Next is the routine you participate in that makes up the habit.

- **Reward:** Lastly, there is some form of reward your brain feels that makes you want to repeat this habit.

Habits aren't good or bad; it's the result of these habits that can make a difference.

Most habits follow this cycle of cue, routine, and reward. Let's look at some examples of this cycle. Below is a table with different cues, routines, and rewards to help you understand what a habit looks like. There are a few boxes left blank so you can fill them in with your habits. Reflect on different cues, routines, and rewards to see how habits may keep unfolding in your life.

Cue	Routine	Reward
see an ad for a candy bar	buy and eat the candy bar	sugar rush and satisfied craving
the morning alarm	brush your teeth and take a shower	being prepared for the day
the school day ends	go for a jog	feeling refreshed (long-term reward of supported health)

When it comes to eating UPFs, the reward is often instant, but the results aren't as obvious, like brain fog or mood swings. Reworking our habits is all about identifying our current routines and then noticing the cue so we can make changes. Then, we can find habits that give us better long-term rewards.

Activity: Your Habits

Below is a table you can utilize to help you better reflect on your habits. In the first box, identify the current habits you've already begun to identify. As you become more reflective, you will start to notice more habits that you might not have even realized were such a big part of your life. Start with the main habits you'd like to change, and keep it focused on eating habits.

In the second box, discuss where you're getting most of your nutrition. Is this from fast-food meals, home-cooked dinners, or the school cafeteria?

In the next two boxes, write down your motivation and main goal. You might have a few goals or points of motivation but try to narrow it down to one so you have a solid foundation to grow from.

My current habits:	•
	•
	•
My main sources of nutrition:	•
	•
	•
My biggest motivating factor is...	
My main goal is...	

Exercise: Mind, Body, Spirit

Changing habits is easier when we put intention behind that change. To help you strengthen your motivating factors and intentions, it's important to see all the ways this habit impacts your mind, body, and spirit:

- **My Habit:** In the first column, write down your different habits related to UPFs, and any others that might impact your mood, appetite, and lifestyle.

- **My Mind:** In the second column, note all the effects this habit has on your mind. What thoughts and feelings do you have before, during, and after performing the routine?

- **My Body:** In the third column, notice any physical sensations associated with this habit, such as body aches, or discomfort in your stomach or chest.

- **My Spirit:** In the fourth column, note how UPFs impact your spirit, (i.e. your motivation, happiness, or sense of fulfillment).

The first one is filled out for you as an example. Use the rest of the boxes to raise awareness of your current habits.

My Habit	My Mind	My Body	My Spirit
I tend to overeat snacks while binge-watching my favorite shows at night.	I often don't have much awareness during this time and mindlessly snack. My thoughts make me want to keep snacking while watching TV.	After overeating at night, I find it hard to get up and feel energized, and struggle with digestion issues from eating too much sugar.	I usually feel disappointed with myself, but it's hard to find the motivation to stop because it's become such a habit.

Awareness of your habits can inspire you to make better choices for your health. Once you see just how impactful your habits have been, you'll realize just how important it is to make changes that prioritize your wellness.

Reflection

What do you know so far about different kinds of ultra-processed foods?

What has motivated you to learn more about different types of foods?

What does health mean to you?

What are some things you're hoping to learn about UPFs?

What is one main thing that keeps you from being able to make better changes?

Differentiating Foods

What qualifies a UPF from a minimally processed or unprocessed food? Let's take a look.

Unprocessed	Processed	Ultra-Processed
<ul><li>no added ingredients</li><li>no or very little alteration from the original state of the food</li></ul>	<ul><li>one or more ingredients may have been added</li><li>slight processing such as cooking, washing, or preserving has altered the food</li></ul>	<ul><li>multiple ingredients and additives used to change the color, texture, flavor, or shelf-life of the food</li><li>multiple stages of processing have altered the food from its original state</li></ul>

Example Foods	Example Foods	Example Foods
• whole fruits and veggies, like apples or carrots • eggs • nuts or seeds	• canned fruits and vegetables • pickled or jarred fruits and vegetables • some breads, cheeses, and other dairy products	• soda • candy • chips • packaged cookies • energy drinks • gluten-free pasta

It's not always about the ingredients; the processing stage is just as important to your health. For example, some processed foods may not be absorbed as easily in the body when they are broken down, cooked, or mixed with other ingredients.

Let's take a look at a few more examples to help you better understand the impact of UPFs:

Type of Process or Additive	Why It's Harmful
Sodium nitrite: This is a preservative often used in packaged and processed meats like deli meat, hot dogs, bacon, sausages, pepperoni, and more.	This is a known carcinogen, meaning it increases cancer risk. They also increase heart disease risk as well as diabetes.
Sodium benzoate: This extends shelf-life, helping foods avoid spoiling or growing mold. You'll find it in bottled or jarred ultra-processed foods.	Another known carcinogen that can negatively impact health. It may also cause inflammation and impact appetite control.
Aspartame: This is a popular sugar alternative found in many drinks, such as energy drinks, sports hydration drinks, and diet or zero-sugar sodas.	Aspartame affects appetite and metabolism, which may lead to cravings or overeating.
Food coloring: This is used to make food look better. It's often found in foods like candy or drinks, but may also be used in food like yogurt or salad dressing to	Certain food dyes may cause: • allergic reaction

make it appear more appealing.	• hyperactivity in children • thyroid issues
Emulsifiers: These help keep foods together so they don't separate, such as processed liquids and other beverages.	Some emulsifiers may cause inflammation and impact overall gut health.
Maltodextrin: This is used to help thicken food and make products more shelf-stable, elongating their shelf-life.	Maltodextrin is found in many ultra-processed foods and is known for causing weight gain and increased blood sugar.

These common additives are just a few of many found in UPFs that negatively impact your health.

Activity: Common Foods

For this activity, the left-hand column represents food that is unprocessed, minimally processed, processed, or ultra-processed.

In the right column, guess which category you think this food belongs in. Don't research the answers just yet. This is just to help you assess what you might know or not know about foods thus far.

After completion, look at the answer key to check your responses.

Food	Unprocessed, Minimally Processed, Processed, or Ultra-Processed?
Bottled sweetened iced coffee with milk	
Flavored breakfast cereal	
Peanut butter	
Raw chicken	
Lunch meat	
Bananas	
Olive oil	
Ground black pepper	
Water mix-ins/flavor packets	
Walnuts	
Canned tuna	
Energy drink	

Answer Key: Below are the foods listed above in their appropriate category so you can compare your answers.

Unprocessed	Minimally Processed	Processed	Ultra-Processed
• bananas • walnuts • raw chicken	• olive oil • ground black pepper	• peanut butter* • canned tuna	• bottled iced coffee • flavored breakfast cereal • lunch meat • water mix-ins/flavor packets • energy drink

This depends on the brand, but it is typically processed as it's mixed with other ingredients.

Exercise: Stages of UPFs

Whole foods can go a long way. What starts as an apple can become something completely different by the time it's ultra-processed.

For this exercise, identify a whole food, and come up with ways that it might be available in the four categories. The first few are filled out for you as an example:

Food	Unprocessed	Minimally Processed	Processed	Ultra-processed
Apple	Whole apple	Dried apples	Applesauce	Apple soda
Carrot	Whole carrot	Washed carrots	Canned carrots	Packaged carrot cake

Reflection

Now that you have a better sense of what UPFs are, how often do you find yourself eating them?

What has surprised you most about UPFs?

What side effects have you noticed after eating different types of UPFs?

What is a food you thought wouldn't be a UPF, but is?

What has surprised you most when learning about different food additives?

Comparing the Impact

Only you can decide what you want to eat. Use the comparison table below to help you make better choices. On the left, you'll find some common effects of eating UPFs compared to the common effects of eating unprocessed or minimally processed foods on the right. Seeing this comparison can help you understand just how drastic the difference between certain types of foods may be.

UPFs	Unprocessed or Minimally Processed Foods
Brain fog: UPFs are known to impact cognitive function, making it difficult to focus, learn new information, and process	**Mental clarity:** Supporting the brain means having a diverse range of healthy fats, vitamins, and minerals in your diet.

thoughts and emotions. They also alter our reward system, meaning we are more likely to keep going back for more after consuming them.	Whole and fresh foods, such as fatty fish, nuts, and green, leafy vegetables, regulate hunger, increase concentration, and improve memory.
Lethargy: UPFs often have little nutritional value and are instead filled with sugars. These can provide a short energy rush followed by a crash.	**Energy:** Whole grains such as brown rice or whole wheat bread take longer for the body to digest, allowing you to feel fuller longer while also sustaining energy levels.
Mood swings: Research shows those who eat UPFs have a higher risk of developing depression and anxiety. When UPFs impact our emotions, it impacts our ability to make good choices for our diet, thus contributing to a cycle of eating certain foods.	**Emotional regulation:** When energy levels, focus, and moods are managed, it becomes much easier to handle our thoughts and feelings. High sugar or caffeine content can make us feel more stressed, whereas healthy whole foods support cognitive function.
Health risks: UPFs have over "32 harmful effects to health, including a higher risk of heart disease, cancer, type 2 diabetes, adverse mental health, and early death" (Gregory, 2024).	**Disease and illness prevention:** A balanced diet is a great preventative measure to protect your health as research shows diet notifications can prevent many diseases and illnesses.

Environmental Impact

Beyond our bodies, UPFs negatively impact the environment. Below are some facts about how the environment is damaged, followed by some reflection questions:

- UPFs use a large amount of packaging, leading to excess waste before and after production. Land, water, and energy are required to create and produce UPFs, which can harm both native species and the ecosystem as a whole.

- UPFS contribute to up to 45% of biodiversity loss, in the diet-related category (Cliff, 2022).

- The largest contributors to negative environmental impacts are foods containing palm and soy oils, as well as processed meat. Palm oil production has led to a massive loss of plant and animal species—including rare and endangered species—as it requires the destruction of rainforests. Over 50% of packaged foods consumed in America contain palm oil ("Palm oil," n.d.).

The effects UPFs have on the environment are devastating. When we consume UPFs in a high amount, not only are we hurting our bodies, but we are hurting the world we live in. Diverse animal and plant life is destroyed for the sake of creating these highly addictive, low-nutritional foods, so it's important to recognize these impacts to fuel our motivation to make better choices.

Reflection Questions

Why is it important to reduce UPFs for the sake of the environment?

How important is it to you to protect the universe?

Do you find that you prioritize the environmental impact over the health impact of UPFs?

Activity: UPF Impact

This next activity can help you identify the impact that certain foods have had on your body. Using the guided chart below, fill in what common symptoms you've been experiencing in relation to each part of your body. For each box, close your eyes and tap into how this body part feels. Do you experience any pain or other negative side effects? What about this might you wish to change? Fill in those answers in the empty box next to each body part:

Head: Do you struggle with headaches, brain fog, memory issues, concentration, and focus?	
Energy levels: Do you feel tension, soreness, lethargy, or any other ache in your body?	
Chest/lungs: Do you struggle to regulate your breathing or find that you suffer from chest tightness due to anxiety?	
Stomach and digestion: Do you have irregular bowel movements, stomach aches, or cramping?	
Muscles (arms, legs, etc.): Are you often tired, sore, or struggling to recover from physical activity?	

Exercise: Expanding on Goals

Next up, look back on the first exercise and expand on your goals and motivations:

- Identify more motivating factors you have that will support you on this journey, or break down a big point of motivation into smaller parts.

- What smaller milestones will you need to take to get there? What tasks do you have to complete to reach your goals?

- Last, identify big obstacles, as this will help prepare you for the things to look out for in the future.

Positive and healthy goals will enable you to have a foundation for positive change throughout the remainder of the book.

My Main Goal: _____

Main Motivation	Smaller Milestones	Biggest Obstacles
•	•	•
•	•	•
•	•	•

Reflection

Why is it important for you to make choices that support the environment?

Why is it important for you to set goals?

What are you thinking and feeling right now, and how does that impact what you know about UPFs?

What are some long-term goals you have, and why will making the right choices surrounding food help you get there?

What are the main triggers you will have to look out for?

Chapter 2:
Traversing the World of UPFs

Knowledge is power, but now it's time to expand on what you've learned and investigate UPFs further to control their impact on you. Habit change happens much easier when it's done in small steps. While you might set a goal for yourself, it's important to keep repeating the process of your routines and rituals until that habit is established.

Attach your habits to one another as well. When you decide to avoid a UPF, use that decision to inspire you to try another small habit, like reading a book or going for a jog.

UPFs may be difficult to resist because they trigger our reward system; however, implementing new habits will give you fresh ways of activating that reward system, thus reinforcing better decisions.

Finding Power to Break Habits

Why are habits so hard to break?

- Habits are repeated cycles, so it can be hard for us to break those patterns, especially the more we repeat them.

- Habits can be automatic and we might start the cycle without realizing we are.

- Habits can start due to the many triggers we run into throughout the day, so avoiding those triggers helps reduce the impact of the habit.

Why are UPFs so addicting?

- UPFs have high fat and sugar content, providing our brains with good feelings when consumed.

- UPFs are loaded with food coloring and artificial flavors that make them tastier and seemingly more appealing.

- UPFs rely on marketing tactics that make them more desirable than traditional whole foods.

Now that you know about the dangers of UPFs and you have started to raise awareness of your habits, let's dive deeper into the main causes driving impulsivity and activating cravings.

Impulsivity

Teens might struggle with impulsivity more than adults due to their brains still developing. In adolescence, cognitive development in decision-making areas occurs. This creates difficulty for teens when foreseeing and understanding the consequences of their actions. Hormone fluctuations may also cause intense mood swings, which can make it hard to stay level-headed. On top of everything, teens simply have less life experience, making it hard to make the right decisions.

That said, it's not impossible for a teen to control impulses! You simply have to remember to take extra steps when making smart choices for your future. Use the chart below to help you understand how you can avoid your most intense urges, reducing the likelihood of UPF consumption.

How to Avoid Intense Urges:

- Use mindfulness to keep you grounded in the moment and prevent indulging in UPFs. Do a quick body scan to notice how you are feeling by traveling from the top of your head to the bottom of your feet.

- Find a distraction when you have a craving. It should be something that absorbs your mind, like a book or a good movie. If you redirect your focus, it can be easier to say no to impulses.

- Drink water and do a breathing exercise. Breathe in through your nose as you count to five, and then breathe out through your mouth as you count down from five. Sip water and focus on the present to help you have more control over impulses.

Activity: Your Cravings

Cravings are easily conquered when we break them down and understand them on a deeper level. The worksheet below can help you understand your cravings.

Instructions:

1. Identify your biggest cravings. What food do you find hard to resist?

2. Label the incident, emotion, thought, or feeling at the time of the craving that might be causing the craving to occur.

3. Think of some alternatives you could eat that could satisfy any hunger cues without being ultra-processed.

4. Think of an alternative activity you could do to avoid eating if you find that you're not actually hungry.

Craving	Trigger	Alternative Food	Alternative Activity
chips	boredom	sliced carrots	read
cookie	need for something sweet	banana	do a craft

This helps slow cravings so you can understand them better. Keep in mind that you don't have to ignore hunger cues; eat something wholesome if you find that you are hungry. However, if you find you're not hungry and you're eating for other reasons, having an activity in mind will remind you to focus your attention elsewhere.

Exercise: UPF Map

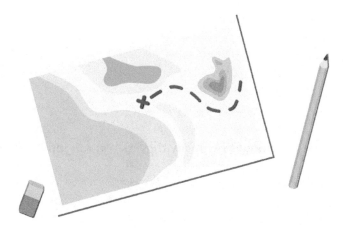

For this exercise, create a map of all the triggers you run into that can hinder progress and kickstart cravings. This will help you reroute your day to make it easier to make healthy choices.

To practice this exercise, create a map connecting all of the places you go throughout the day. Once completed, highlight any areas where you run into UPFs, or UPF triggers, such as advertisements. Once you're done, review these locations to see if there is any way to reroute your day to avoid or reduce temptations. For example, maybe you can walk through the park on your way home from school rather than pass by a street with a convenience store. This map will help you see how many UPF temptations you run into throughout the day.

Reflection

Why do you think you've been struggling to avoid UPFs?

What surprises you most about how many triggers you run into throughout the day?

What are some of your biggest habits surrounding UPFs?

Which triggers are hardest for you to avoid?

Have you noticed any triggers now that you didn't realize were so triggering in the past?

Learning Label Language

Reading labels can be confusing. This is true especially for UPFs because we might not know what some ingredients are, or what certain words even mean.

For example, sugar has many different names and appears on an ingredient list under other titles. The table below can help you recognize some ingredients to look out for alongside other names they may be listed under.

Remember, not all ingredients are harmful, as things like salt and sugar are needed in our diet in some capacity; the right *kind* is what's important. For example, fruits and vegetables contain **naturally derived** salts and sugars that are good for you in moderation. Foods like packaged candy and microwavable meals contain **added** sugar and salt that can pose health risks when consumed in excess. For the sake of this table, foods like salt and sugar are used in an ultra-processed food context to help you differentiate added ingredients.

Ingredient	Alternative Names	Why It's Harmful
Sugar: often added to make food more satisfying to eat, taste better, and last longer	• fructose • sucrose • dextrose/dextrin • maltose	Added sugar impacts every part of the body, from weight management to cognitive function.
Salt: added to foods to preserve, enhance flavor, and make them more enticing to eat	• sodium nitrite • sodium phosphate • sodium bicarbonate • sodium benzoate	Too much salt poses health risks such as heart disease, high blood pressure, and stroke susceptibility.
Preservatives: extend the shelf-life of certain foods and prevent the growth of mold or bacteria	• butylated hydroxytoluene • propyl gallate • butylated hydroxyanisole • propylparaben	These are often potentially carcinogenic, harm development, and disrupt hormone production.
Food dyes: used to enhance the appearance of certain foods	• blue 1 • red 40 • yellow 5 and 6 • green 3	Food dyes may impact mood and focus, and increase cancer risk.
Stabilizers (or emulsifiers): prevent food from separating, improving its appearance and texture	• sodium carboxymethyl cellulose • xanthan gum • carrageenan • polysorbate-80	These can impact the digestive system and may harm the body's microbiome.

Activity: UPF Ingredients

Learning about UPF ingredients is an ongoing process, so it's important to know how to research various ingredients to help you stay informed. Below is a worksheet to conduct some research on top UPF foods. To give you inspiration for UPFs, open up a food delivery or grocery shopping app and notice any brands or ads that appear first. Write these UPFs down. For example, you might get an ad for a fried chicken restaurant chain. What ingredients are found in their dipping sauces? If you head to a store, maybe you're presented with a big display of different candies. What ingredients are found in those?

For each UPF you find, write down three ingredients you don't recognize and research them to see their impact.

Ultra-Processed Food	Ingredients	Why It's Harmful
	1. 2. 3.	
	1. 2. 3.	
	1. 2. 3.	
	1. 2. 3.	
	1.	

	2.		
	3.		

Exercise: Ingredient Comparison

For this worksheet, your next challenge is to look up various recipes for the same type of product.

Head to your local grocery store again, or use shopping apps on your phone, and compare various ingredients of different types of foods with similar products. For example, in the first row, find a popular type of salad dressing sold in the store.

Next, see if there is a less processed version of the product. Perhaps one found in the produce section of your grocery store. Also, certain foods labeled as organic may have fewer additives than nonorganic. If you can't find one that is processed, find an alternative instead.

Lastly, research a homemade recipe made with whole foods, and list the top three ingredients. What differences do you notice among these ingredients? What surprises you most about your findings?

Type of Food	Ultra-Processed	Processed/ Alternative	Homemade Recipe
Salad Dressing	1. 2. 3.	1. 2. 3.	1. 2. 3.
Pasta Sauce	1. 2. 3.	1. 2. 3.	1. 2. 3.
Cupcake	1. 2. 3.	1. 2. 3.	1. 2. 3.

Orange Juice	1. 2. 3.	1. 2. 3.	1. 2. 3.
Cereal	1. 2. 3.	1. 2. 3.	1. 2. 3.
	1. 2. 3.	1. 2. 3.	1. 2. 3.
	1. 2. 3.	1. 2. 3.	1. 2. 3.
	1. 2. 3.	1. 2. 3.	1. 2. 3.
	1. 2. 3.	1. 2. 3.	1. 2. 3.
	1. 2. 3.	1. 2. 3.	1. 2. 3.

Reflection

What have you learned so far about exploring labels?

Why do you think it's important to read ingredient lists?

Reflect on common ingredients you might've been consuming. What impact has this had on you?

What do you plan to do in the future to avoid these ingredients?

What has surprised you most about food labels?

Staying One Step Ahead

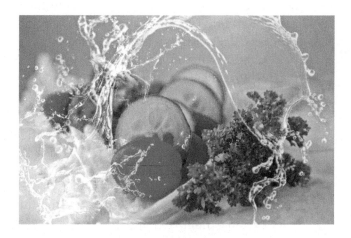

Teens are a targeted group of buyers for many UPF marketing companies. Brands take advantage of a teenager's struggle with impulse control. Teens are more easily influenced by things like celebrity endorsements and other marketing tactics. Staying one step ahead of UPF cravings requires that we identify these predatory marketing tactics to reduce their impact. Below is a table of different marketing tactics, what they look like, and examples you might've seen before:

Marketing Tactic	Description	Examples
Endorsements	Celebrity endorsements are often used to connect a product to a figure you trust or admire.	• a pop star selling a drink • a sports team promoting a snack
Urgency	Brands will use words like "limited edition" or "while supplies last" to instill an urgent feeling in consumers, making them feel like they need to buy something ASAP.	• limited edition flavors for drinks and candy • rare or collectible items associated with snacks
Colorful images	Advertisements with happy, well-dressed people in sunny, exciting places make a product seem more intriguing.	• people celebrating in an advertisement all sharing the same type of soda • labels with intricate

		designs
User-generated	Some companies encourage consumers to create their own content around certain products. This creates a sense of community around a product, urging consumers to join in on trends.	• sharing a picture of a product on social media using a certain hashtag • videos of people trying or taste-testing new products
Influencer	Influencers are very powerful in persuading people to make purchases. An influencer trying a product or even just having it in the background of a vlog might seem genuine but are most likely an ad.	• an influencer sharing a drink they have all the time • an influencer giving followers discount codes for certain products
Loyalty and rewards	Many brands have reward programs, so if you spend a certain amount of money, you'll get points that can be used to make more purchases.	• buy three items, get one free deal • join a rewards program to get discounts in your email

Activity: Decoding Marketing

Now that you know some of the marketing tactics used against you, let's take a look at some of your top brands and their ads. In the left column, write down your favorite

UPF brands. Then, head to their social media pages and look at some of the content they post. What ads do you see? Check out hashtags to see if any celebrities or influencers are also a part of the marketing scheme.

My Top Brands:	Their Marketing Strategy:

Now, step away from some of your favorite brands and look at other brands you're exposed to simply by going to the store or scrolling social media.

UPFs at the Store or Online:	Their Marketing Strategy:

For the last part of this activity, track how many ads you see a week. Start in the morning, and mark a tally for each time you see an ad in the corresponding column. Then, write some of the sources of these ads, such as social media, on TV, or other physical ads out in the world (i.e. billboards, flyers, posters).

Day	Morning	Afternoon	Night	Common Ad Sources:
Monday				
Tuesday				
Wednesday				
Thursday				
Friday				
Saturday				
Sunday				

After you've finished tracking how many ads you've seen, answer the following:

- Ad count total: _____

- Most common time of day to see ads: _____

- Most common source for ads: _____

Take some time to reflect on this experience and write your thoughts below. What did you learn about ads in this process? What steps can you take in the future to reduce the amount of ads you see?

Exercise: Avoiding Common Tricks

Ads can be easier to spot the more you familiarize yourself with common advertising tactics. For this last part of the exercise, let's explore misleading phrases that trick you into thinking a product is healthier than it is.

Listed in the left column are misleading phrases used to trick you into thinking you are healthy. On the right is some information about why this may actually indicate a food is a UPF. Take some time to look around your local store or use a food delivery app to find examples of products that contain these words.

Misleading Phrase	The Truth
"sugar-free" My product examples: • • •	While it's good to avoid excess sugar, reaching for "sugar-free" products might not be the healthiest choice to make. "Sugar-free" foods may contain artificial sweeteners, dyes, and other additives which are unfavorable choices for your health.

"plant milk" My product examples: • • •	Plant milks often contain additives that negate any health benefits they provide. The word "plant" might make it seem like these are healthier alternatives to dairy milk, but they may contain harmful ingredients.
"low-calorie" My product examples: • • •	There is no significant health advantage associated with "low-calorie" foods. They are usually just smaller portions. Foods labeled "low-calorie" may still contain preservatives and additives that are harmful when consumed in excess.
"natural" My product examples: • •	There are no FDA regulations on what can be given a "natural" label. Something that may contain a natural ingredient, such as natural food coloring, doesn't mean it is free of "unnatural" ingredients, like excess sugar or preservatives.
"gluten-free" My product examples: • •	Gluten-free doesn't always mean something is healthier. While it may not contain gluten, which can be harmful to those who have gluten allergies, there are likely other ingredients in these products that make them UPFs.

Reflection

How might you have been influenced in the past by things you saw online?

What are the biggest sources of ads you're exposed to?

What common strategies of advertisements do you often see?

What impacts have advertisements had on you?

What has been the most shocking when learning about advertising tactics?

Chapter 3:
Maximizing Your Mindset

Beating the influence of UPFs is all about creating the right mindset to avoid cravings and stay grounded for mindful eating. Your body doesn't *need* UPFs, but the many influences around us and thoughts in our head can make it feel that way. Let's take a look at some final reminders and tips to maximize your mindset so you can stay focused and one step ahead of UPFs.

Balance Is the Key

Sometimes when trying out a new eating habit, people tend to develop an all-or-nothing mindset, which can hinder progress. They believe that they must have a perfectly healthy diet, and if they eat something unhealthy, they should give up, only to have to start again later on. That's not the case! You can live a healthy, wholesome lifestyle, and still indulge occasionally.

Restricting foods to an extreme level can make them even more tempting. If you tell yourself you're not allowed to have chips, candy, and soda, it could only make you crave them more!

The fluctuation of guilt and shame as you indulge in certain foods can cause even more intense emotions that are hard to deal with. These mood swings might lead to cravings, which add to the stress you're already feeling.

UPFs are inescapable, so there may be occasions when it's okay to indulge, like a party or holiday. While it's always best to limit your UPF intake, give yourself some grace to avoid negative emotions attached to eating.

Focus on balance, as this will prevent you from demonizing or fearing certain foods, and maintain mindfulness over the habits you're forming.

It's also important to maintain balance in terms of replacing foods you take away. If you remove snacks and other UPFs from your diet, replace them with healthier options to maintain balance. If you restrict and remove, it becomes harder to maintain the right mindset.

Activity: Cravings Assessment

Below are five statements about cravings. Rank each statement starting with 1 for the statement you relate to the most, and 5 for the one that you don't.

Your Ranking	Statement
	I tend to snack the most when I am bored, procrastinating, and simply need something to do.
	I find it hard to avoid giving in to cravings when I'm at an event or in public.
	Snacking is a way for me to relieve stress and it provides me with comfort.
	I often eat snacks at night when watching TV or using social media.
	I overeat often when I am feeling tired or have little sleep and need a pick-me-up.

Now, assess your results. Within each of these five statements is a core issue that needs to be addressed, thus allowing you to better implement changes into your lifestyle.

- The first statement shows that the core issue is boredom or avoidance. Food may become an escape, so it's crucial to notice if you are trying to procrastinate or alleviate boredom when giving in to cravings.

- In the second statement, the root issue is a lack of impulse control. You may find it hard to avoid giving in to cravings in situations that provide excess temptation. If this is the case, practice mindfulness to strengthen your impulse control.

- When food becomes a comfort, it's hard to avoid giving in to those temptations. If you find yourself leaning on food for stress relief, it's time to address the issues that are stressing you out.

- In the fourth statement, the problem here is that eating has become a habitual part of a routine. It's time to break the ritual and have an alternative hobby to have on hand at night. Perhaps you can take up crocheting or cross-stitching and do this while watching TV instead of snacking.

- Lastly, if you find that your energy levels are a big trigger for overeating UPFs, it may be important to reflect on your overall health. Do you need to get more sleep each night to feel refreshed? You might even find you have a vitamin deficiency, so be proactive about reflecting on your health.

You might relate to all statements, and that's understandable! UPFs are hard to avoid. Reflecting on your biggest triggers further enables you to overcome your biggest habits.

Exercise: Portion Picture

Maintaining a balanced, healthy lifestyle is all about mindful eating. Mindful eating focuses on listening to your body when eating and living in the moment. Mindful eating keeps us present, allowing us to have more control over our impulses.

One element that can help amplify mindful eating is to reflect on portion sizes. Often, the issue with UPFs is the amount in which they might be consumed. An occasional soda or fast food meal isn't life-threatening, but consuming this repeatedly throughout the week can pose health risks.

To help you maintain more control over how much you're eating let's take a look at different portion sizes.

1. To start, grab a UPF you might still have around your house and measure out the actual portion size. Read the ingredient label and see what the recommended portion size is. This will help provide you with a visual image of how much you should be eating (or less!).

2. Next, take that portion, and transfer it into three different types of containers: one small, one medium, and one large. This will encourage you to be more mindful of the portions you are eating to maintain balance surrounding

UPFs. You might be surprised to see how big or how little a portion looks based on the container. Sometimes it can be easy to eat a bag of chips in one sitting when we aren't mindful of how many chips we're actually eating.

UPFs like cereal and chips often have small portion sizes on their nutrition labels. Sometimes, you might read the labels and feel surprised that there aren't many calories or that there's a low sugar content. However, most of the time, a much higher amount is actually consumed when we're eating because we don't realize just how small those portions are, leading to excessive calorie consumption. This exercise serves to give you a better sense of how much UPFs you consume and improves your relationship with portion size.

Reflection

What surprised you most after you measured out the portion size?

How many of the portions do you often eat in one sitting?

Do you feel as though you've been overeating UPFs?

How do your cravings trigger a tendency to overeat?

What might be stopping you from implementing better habits?

Raising Awareness

Mindfulness is the most effective way to ensure that awareness is raised over eating habits. Mindfulness raises our awareness of our emotions, both past and present. This allows us to act accordingly.

If you are feeling anxious or struggle with intense emotions, you might be more likely to react to impulses and urges that hinder progress and set you back. Mindfulness grounds you in the present so you can better respond to hunger cues or craving triggers and give more focus to healthier decisions.

Mindfulness is a tool to keep us present in the moment so we are one step ahead of our biggest cravings. One type of mindfulness is intuitive eating. This allows you to recognize hunger cues and act accordingly.

Activity: Intuitive Eating

Intuitive Eating Tips

Let go of extreme restrictions: Let yourself eat when you are hungry and don't deny your body's signals. If you ignore hunger cues, you may develop a tendency to ignore cues when you are full as well.

- **Stop eating once hunger dissipates:** You don't have to finish your plate. It's hard to toss food because we might feel wasteful. However, your body isn't a waste receptacle either; it's better to throw food in the trash than to eat it just out of fear of waste.

- **Give yourself smaller portions:** Start with a small portion and wait a moment after you eat to practice listening to your body. If you still feel hungry, you can always get more. This encourages us to listen to our body and slow down rather than eat large portions.

- **Drink water with every meal:** Even if you're indulging in another beverage, have water with your meals to help with digestion. This will give you a truer sense of fullness.

- **Become friends with yourself:** Food is not the enemy, nor is your body. Treat your body with kindness as this will help you better listen to it and provide it with nourishment rather than restrict foods as a means of punishment.

Now, use these tips to practice intuitive eating for one week. Below are seven tables to help you keep track of different elements of your hunger throughout the week. Fill out one each day to help you strengthen your ability to eat intuitively.

- **My Hunger Level:** In the first column, assess your hunger level before eating. Rate this between 1 and 10. This will help slow you down so you have to be more reflective on your eating habits.

- **My Emotions:** Take a moment to think about your emotions. Is there an emotion driving you right now, like stress or boredom? Slowing down and assessing your feelings can strengthen your ability to notice some of the biggest triggers driving your decisions.

- **Rating:** Use this to help you identify how intuitive you are feeling with your choices. For example, if you gave in to cravings due to stressful emotions even though you weren't hungry, your rating might be a 1. If you listened to your body when you weren't hungry and chose to do a hobby instead of eat, you might give yourself a 10. There are no right or wrong answers—this rating simply serves as an encouragement to reflect on the practice of intuitive eating.

Monday	My Hunger Level	My Emotions	Rating
Morning			
Afternoon			
Night			

Tuesday	My Hunger Level	My Emotions	Rating
Morning			
Afternoon			
Night			

Wednesday	My Hunger Level	My Emotions	Rating
Morning			
Afternoon			
Night			

Thursday	My Hunger Level	My Emotions	Rating
Morning			
Afternoon			
Night			

Friday	My Hunger Level	My Emotions	Rating
Morning			
Afternoon			
Night			

Saturday	My Hunger Level	My Emotions	Rating
Morning			
Afternoon			
Night			

Sunday	My Hunger Level	My Emotions	Rating
Morning			
Afternoon			
Night			

Exercise: Whole Food Mindfulness

Mindful eating means slowing down and enjoying our food on all levels. For this exercise, pick a whole fruit or vegetable that you enjoy. Then, slowly go through the process of eating it. Take time to describe what it looks, feels, smells, tastes, and sounds like as you eat. Go through your answers and record your findings in the corresponding columns below.

My food: _____

Sight	Touch	Smell	Taste	Sound

My food: _____

Sight	Touch	Smell	Taste	Sound

My food: _____

Sight	Touch	Smell	Taste	Sound

Reflection

Do you feel as though you mindfully or mindlessly eat, and why?

What does being mindful look like to you?

What are some of the most influential eating habits you have in your life?

What sensations do you feel when you're hungry?

How often do you believe you listen to your body's hunger or fullness cues?

Experimenting With Alternatives

We don't have to give up all of our favorite foods to live happier lives. Embarking on a healthy journey of choosing certain foods over others can be daunting for anyone, but especially for a teen.

You may be wondering: *Does this mean I can never eat pizza or potato chips again?* You don't have to give up all the foods you love! The point of giving up UPFs and reducing how much you eat them is to help you focus on healthy, wholesome ingredients that support better nutrition. Eat all the foods you love—just focus on swapping out certain ingredients and choosing the kinds that provide your body with nutrition rather than harmful additives.

Activity: Better Replacements

For this activity, identify some common UPFs you enjoy eating. Then, think of some alternative replacements. The first few are filled out for you.

Common UPF	Better Replacement
Potato chips	<ul><li>raw, sliced veggies with hummus</li><li>whole kernel popcorn or nuts</li></ul>
Ice cream	<ul><li>homemade sorbet</li><li>yogurt with fruit topping</li></ul>

Exercise: Homemade Versions

Cooking is a great way to help you repair your relationship with food and get more excited about different culinary creations. A great way to explore cooking is by replicating your favorite foods, snacks, and treats. For this exercise, you're challenged to find your favorite UPF and make a homemade version:

1. Identify your favorite fast food or UPF. This might be a meal, a drink, or a simple snack.

2. Find an alternative recipe online to try. Search Google and social media for recipes. If you pick a popular food, chances are, there's a recipe to replicate it!

3. Use videos to learn how to make different meals and ingredients with some inspiration for changing things up. Just ensure the recipes you follow are using whole ingredients.

Cooking is a learning process, so don't be discouraged if you don't fall in love with your first recipe! Keep trying new things and your skills will improve.

After you make your food, reflect on the questions below:

- What did you learn in this experience?

- Did you find that the homemade version was better?

- What are some more recipes you want to experiment with in the future?

Reflection

Going forward, what plans do you have in place to manage your biggest cravings?

What plans do you have in place for the future to keep making positive changes?

Think back on the first reflection questions. Do you notice any changes?

What are the most valuable insights you've gained throughout this workbook?

What has been the biggest challenge so far?

Chapter 4:
Six-Week Action Plan

Now it's time to take everything you've learned and take action! Below is a six-week action plan to help you cut back on ultra-processed foods and find replacements for healthier living. With this step-by-step process, you'll discover how to raise awareness over the food choices you've been making and empower yourself to make better decisions going forward.

You'll find six different tables below, one for each week. Each table has seven goals that will help you build simple habits and changes that will accumulate for bigger results over the six weeks. In the left column are daily goals, and on the right is a reflection section.

In this reflection section, discuss the goal and why it helps make positive changes in your life. If you're not sure what to write about in your reflection, consider these things:

- the difficulty level of the goal

- any challenges you ran into along the way

- what you learned during the process

- what you learned after when reflecting on the goal

- why you believe this goal is important

These steps can help you make the most of this six-week plan and easily make long-lasting, positive changes.

You can complete this challenge while doing the other activities and exercises in the book, or you can save this for after. The choice is yours—remember, the decisions you make now will impact your success in the future!

Week One: Raise Awareness

The first step in reducing ultra-processed food consumption is noticing how it has infiltrated your life and habits.

Monday Goal	Today's Reflection
Take a walk through your kitchen and notice any ultra-processed foods.	

Tuesday Goal	Today's Reflection
Scroll through your three most used social media apps for 30 minutes each, and notice any ads for ultra-processed foods.	

Wednesday Goal	Today's Reflection
Notice any cravings you experience for different ultra-processed foods.	

Thursday Goal	Today's Reflection
Raise awareness of the physical sensations you feel after eating ultra-processed foods, and how this impacts your body.	

Friday Goal	Today's Reflection
Head to the grocery store and study some ultra-processed foods firsthand.	

Saturday Goal	Today's Reflection
Identify some of the thoughts or urges you have before eating ultra-processed foods.	

Sunday Goal	Today's Reflection
Review the weekly goals and reflect on what you learned the most about ultra-processed foods.	

Week Two: Build Motivation

Now that you have a better understanding of ultra-processed foods, discover some motivating factors that will help you stay on track.

Monday Goal	Today's Reflection
Identify why you want to quit eating ultra-processed foods and discuss why it's important to you.	

Tuesday Goal	Today's Reflection
Label some of the negative side effects you've personally experienced from ultra-processed food consumption.	

Wednesday Goal	Today's Reflection
Reflect on how ultra-processed foods may impact the world as a whole.	

Thursday Goal	Today's Reflection
Create a personal goal for quitting ultra-processed foods.	

Friday Goal	Today's Reflection
Label the steps you will need to take to reach this goal.	

Saturday Goal	Today's Reflection
Find an accountability partner or friend who can keep you motivated.	

Sunday Goal	Today's Reflection
Reflect on what you've learned throughout this week, and expand on your biggest point of motivation.	

Week Three: Discover Replacements

The best way to stop old habits is to replace them with new ones!

Monday Goal	Today's Reflection
Research a recipe for a replacement version of your favorite ultra-processed food.	

Tuesday Goal	Today's Reflection
Buy the ingredients for this recipe.	

Wednesday Goal	Today's Reflection
Make this recipe, and reflect on the entire process, including your feelings when shopping and cooking.	

Thursday Goal	Today's Reflection
Identify any ultra-processed foods you've eaten this week, and label why it was difficult to avoid them.	

Friday Goal	Today's Reflection
Create an entire meal based around minimally processed foods, and prepare to make it this weekend.	

Saturday Goal	Today's Reflection
Cook a minimally processed meal and write about your experiences.	

Sunday Goal	Today's Reflection
Reflect on how you're feeling this week, and what you learned the most about finding replacements for ultra-processed foods.	

Week Four: Reduce Consumption

The only way to build better goals is to start the process of cutting ultra-processed foods out of your life.

Monday Goal	Today's Reflection
Write down every time you notice yourself craving an ultra-processed food.	

Tuesday Goal	Today's Reflection
Repeat Monday's goal, and identify the biggest trigger for these cravings.	

Wednesday Goal	Today's Reflection
Limit yourself to three forms of ultra-processed foods for the day (one for each meal).	

Thursday Goal	Today's Reflection
Limit yourself to two forms of ultra-processed foods for the day.	

Friday Goal	Today's Reflection
Discuss the challenges with limiting ultra-processed foods so far, and identify any motivations you have to continue this limitation.	

Saturday Goal	Today's Reflection
Challenge yourself to avoid ultra-processed foods for the weekend.	

Sunday Goal	Today's Reflection
Discuss the difficulty of ultra-processed food limitation and any other challenges you faced this weekend.	

Week Five: Confront Habits

Now that you're nearing the end of this action plan, the goal is to cut out ultra-processed foods altogether. However, you may still run into them occasionally, so this plan will help you stay on track and learn from the process.

Monday Goal	Today's Reflection
Challenge yourself to avoid ultra-processed foods for the week, and identify your biggest limitations.	

Tuesday Goal	Today's Reflection
Discuss your most common triggers, and for each, identify a way you can avoid this trigger.	

Wednesday Goal	Today's Reflection
Take time to reflect on how you're feeling now that you've limited ultra-processed food consumption.	
Thursday Goal	**Today's Reflection**
Write down any ultra-processed food you've eaten this week, and why it was difficult to avoid them.	
Friday Goal	**Today's Reflection**
Reflect on how you're feeling overall, and what types of limitations you've been able to put in place.	
Saturday Goal	**Today's Reflection**
Repeat last week's challenge and try to go through the weekend without eating ultra-processed foods.	
Sunday Goal	**Today's Reflection**
Reflect on how you're feeling now versus how you were feeling in week one, and identify any major changes.	

Week Six: Find Growth

Growth never stops, so build a future to support more positive change.

Monday Goal	Today's Reflection
Identify a long-term goal you have for your health. Discuss why giving up ultra-processed foods is important for this.	

Tuesday Goal	Today's Reflection
Reflect on the previous weeks and identify the biggest challenges of avoiding ultra-processed foods.	

Wednesday Goal	Today's Reflection
Recognize the things that motivated you the most, and label how you will be able to continue to build on this.	

Thursday Goal	Today's Reflection
Create a list of reminders that will help you stay motivated after you finish this six-week challenge.	

Friday Goal	**Today's Reflection**
Reflect on a time during this process when you almost gave up, and discuss how you were able to find strength.	
Saturday Goal	**Today's Reflection**
Discuss what has been your biggest success during this process, and what helped you succeed.	
Sunday Goal	**Today's Reflection**
Celebrate your success and commend yourself for any major progress you've made in this process.	

Final Reminders

Your future is built by each decision you make. The days ahead are determined by what choices you face for your health, education, happiness, and overall well-being. The best way to take power over the years ahead is by making informed and wise choices to ensure the best version of you thrives. Everything in your life connects, so if your health is struggling, the rest of you might too. By following this action plan to make the process of habit change seamless, you'll discover the power that lies within each choice you make

Bonus:
UPF Worksheets

Below are some additional worksheets to help you reinforce and expand on the information we've covered so far. Follow the instructions to fill them out, then reflect on the worksheet and what you gained in the process. You can use these reflections as journal prompts to help expand on what you learned. Alternatively, you can fill out these worksheets with others, like friends or family, and use the reflections as a point of discussion as you both compare results.

Food Diary

To change a habit, you must first become more aware of how that habit is built. Tracking what you eat for a week is a good way to get a sense of your overall habits.

Instructions

1. Start tracking what you are eating every day. Keep this food diary close by so it's easy to jot down your meals as you have them.

2. Set a timer throughout the day to remind you to check in. You can add a reminder before you go to bed to help you look back on the day and write down everything you ate.

3. If you can, try to write down the amount you ate as well as the type of food.

4. It can also be helpful to write down the time, as this can help you identify any triggers.

5. Consider keeping track of any money spent on these foods to see how much money went toward UPFs.

There are four columns to fill out:

- Breakfast/lunch/dinner: These columns provide space to write down your first, second, and third meal of the day.

- Snacks: Mark snacks or any beverages you eat throughout the day.

Day	Breakfast	Lunch	Dinner	Snacks
Monday				
Tuesday				
Wednesday				
Thursday				
Friday				
Saturday				
Sunday				

Worksheet Reflections

Look through the foods you ate throughout the week, and highlight any UPFs you see.

How often did you consume UPFs throughout the week?

Were there any major patterns you noticed?

What was the total amount you spent on UPFs?

What have you learned about your habits in this process?

Now, use this food diary as inspiration to make changes. These could influence your goals and motivations as you embark on the path of habit change. What triggers can you avoid the following week? Repeat this worksheet after implementing new goals to see in what ways you were able to make changes.

Label Identification

Instructions

Grab your favorite UPF and write it on the line below. Now, look at some of the ingredients, and research what they are, why they're used, and any known side effects that occur with excess consumption.

Research tips:

- When conducting a search online, use websites that end in .org or .edu to ensure they are fact-checked or reviewed by experts.

- Use multiple sources to help back up information.

- Research alternate names for each ingredient to help you find more information.

UPF: _____

Ingredient	Why It's Used	Known Side Effects
		• • •
		• • •
		• • •
		• • •
		• • •

Worksheet Reflections

What surprised you most about some of the ingredients in this UPF?

Out of all the known side effects you've researched, which one is the most concerning for you?

How often do you find yourself consuming this UPF, and in what amount per serving?

Are there any alternative foods or snacks you could think of that would offer a good replacement for this UPF?

What are the biggest triggers present that make you want to consume this UPF?

Why is it important for you to take care of your health and avoid some of the known side effects of this UPF?

How has this activity influenced your perception of this UPF, and do you think it will impact your consumption in the future? Why or why not?

What's in My Cabinet?

Sometimes we don't even realize just how many UPFs we already have. The goal of this worksheet is to help you recognize just how present UPFs are in your life and to shine a light on the things that are considered UPFs that you might not have realized.

There are three columns below:

- **Unprocessed/minimally processed:** In this column, write down any whole foods or any ingredients that are minimally processed, like pepper.

- **Processed:** Use this column to keep track of processed foods such as canned vegetables or pasta. Remember to check the ingredient list if you are unsure if it is processed or ultra-processed.

- **Ultra-processed:** Write down all of the ultra-processed foods you still have in your house.

Go to your cabinet, pantry, fridge, and anywhere else you store food, and categorize everything into the columns below.

Unprocessed and Minimally Processed	Processed	Ultra-Processed

Worksheet Reflections

Evaluate any trends you see in the chart. For example, do you notice that you have a high amount of ultra-processed sweets, or are you more likely to find ultra-processed savory snacks?

Which category is the longest? Why do you think this is?

How frequently do you consume foods from each of these three categories?

Who in your household contributes to the purchase of these various foods?

Do you notice any trends or habits in your family in terms of their consumption of certain foods?

How can these results influence your goals and motivations?

Meal Plans

While you might not have full responsibility over the meals and purchases of your household, you can start to keep track of them, reflect on those habits, and make suggestions or changes as needed.

Below is a meal plan that you and your family can start to follow to help change and build better habits.

First, fill out the table below to help plan different meals throughout the week. Consider meal prepping several portions and repeating meals to help maximize ingredients and keep you prepared throughout the week. Write down any days you plan to go out to eat or order delivery as well, as this will help you strategize what to get so you can avoid UPFs even at restaurants.

Day	Breakfast	Lunch	Dinner
Monday			
Tuesday			

Wednesday			
Thursday			
Friday			
Saturday			
Sunday			

Once that's filled out, use the chart below to assess this plan and ensure you are getting enough minimally or unprocessed foods in your diet. List any vegetables, fruits, grains, and sources of protein in their corresponding column:

Fruits/Vegetables	Whole Grains	Protein/Healthy Fats

It's important to ensure these areas are the focal point of your meals. Avoid planning to incorporate any UPFs into your meal plan.

Lastly, plan ahead for healthy snack and drink options:

Snacks	Drinks

You may ultimately find that you consume UPFs at some point, but if you avoid adding them to your meal plan, it will drastically reduce your consumption.

Planning ahead in this way ensures you have more control over your diet and choices. It helps foster reflection about what you're consuming, thus reducing the likelihood of overconsumption in the future.

Use this as inspiration to keep building, reflecting, and growing your habits for long-term success.

Conclusion

As you move forward and start a new food journey, here are a few things to remember:

- Go at your own pace and reduce feelings of guilt and shame.

- Avoid an all-or-nothing mindset to ensure you stick to your goals.

- Continue research on UPFs to familiarize yourself with them and their impact.

- Don't be afraid to experiment with new foods and recipes—you'll learn what you like and don't like in the process.

- Focus on how you feel and the way different foods impact your thoughts and feelings.

- Reinforce the benefits of eating healthier whole foods and notice how they make your whole body feel.

- Connect the way your mind and body work together and how that impacts the way you think and feel.

Small, gradual changes are always better than big changes that don't last. Think of new ways to expand your knowledge and empower your ability to make informed choices about your diet.

Being a healthy teen means having a healthier future. We can make a difference by encouraging good habits and uplifting others to make positive choices!

If you've enjoyed this workbook, could you please take a moment to leave an Amazon review?

Your feedback helps others find this book and spreads the benefits of healthy eating habits.

Sharing a review helps spread the message and ensures a healthier future for us and the generations that follow.

You can also share the wealth of health by gifting this book to a friend! Embark on a health journal with others around you to **create a system of support and encouragement for change that lasts.**

Start a conversation in the reviews and help others gain access to empowering resources for their health! Thank you for joining this community of empowered living!

***

Did you enjoy this book? Read the next book by C.J.Kindren in the Teen Series:

Find Your Balance: A Teen's Workbook for Mindfulness, Self-Care, and Navigating Change with Courage

>> https://books2read.com/findyourbalance

Life Skills for Teens

Can You Help Please?

Thank you again for reading this book!

Book reviews make all the difference in the discoverability of books.

We would love to hear your thoughts with a quick review on Amazon.

We deeply appreciate this and will read your reviews, thank you!

For your convenience the following QR codes or links take you to directly to the review page at your respective Amazon marketplace:

Amazon.com	Amazon.ca
Amazon.com/review/create-review?&asin=1917353553	Amazon.ca/review/create-review?&asin=1917353553
Amazon.co.uk	Amazon.com.au
Amazon.co.uk/review/create-review?&asin=1917353553	Amazon.com.au/review/create-review?&asin=1917353553

Glossary

Biodiversity: the plants, animals, fungi, and other living things that contribute to a specific environment

Carcinogens: chemicals, ingredients, or other foods known to cause cancer

Consumer: a person who uses a product or service, often in exchange for money

Hyper-palatable: foods with high fat and sugar content that often trigger the brain to crave more.

Marketing: the process of utilizing advertising methods to target and engage consumers

Microbiome: a collection of microorganisms that sustain an environment

Ultra-processed food (UPF): food that has undergone a high level of processing or is mixed with various additives

References

About sodium and health. (n.d.). CDC. https://www.cdc.gov/salt/about/index.html

Added sugars. (n.d.). Illinois Extension. https://eat-move-save.extension.illinois.edu/eat/balance-your-plate/added-sugars

Adolescent development. (n.d.). Cleveland Clinic. https://my.clevelandclinic.org/health/articles/7060-adolescent-development

Ajmera, R. (2018). *12 common food additives—should you avoid them?* Healthline. https://www.healthline.com/nutrition/common-food-additives

Allen, K., Beilin, L., Bremner, A. Herbison., C., Hickling, S., Huang, R., Mori, T., Oddy, W., O'Sullivan, T., Robinson, M. (2012, December). *Low intake of B-vitamins is associated with poor adolescent mental health and behaviour.* Science Direct. https://www.sciencedirect.com/science/article/abs/pii/S0091743512004616

Andrade, G. C., Baker, P., Khandpur, N., Lawrence, M., Leite, F. H. M., Monteiro, C. A., & Anastasiou, K. (2022, March 2). *Ultra-processed foods should be central to global food systems dialogue and action on biodiversity.* NIH. https://pmc.ncbi.nlm.nih.gov/articles/PMC8895941/

Beckett, E. (2024, March 27). *6 'healthy' foods you may not realise are ultra-processed.* BBC Science Focus. https://www.sciencefocus.com/the-human-body/ultra-processed-foods-without-realising

Brown, J. (2021, June 17). *The truth about processed foods' environmental impact.* BBC. https://www.bbc.com/future/article/20210617-the-truth-about-processed-foods-environmental-impact

Calcium: the teen bone builder. (n.d.). Healthy Children. https://www.healthychildren.org/English/ages-stages/teen/nutrition/Pages/Calcium-The-Bone-Builder.aspx

Cliff, C. (2022, August 24). *How bad is ultra-processed food for the planet?* Soil Association. https://www.soilassociation.org/blogs/2022/august/24/how-bad-is-ultra-processed-food-for-the-planet/

Dusenbury, C., Gaziano, T. A., Koplan, J. P., Nugent, R., Puska, P., Willett, W. C. (n.d.). *Prevention of chronic disease by means of diet and lifestyle changes.* NIH. https://www.ncbi.nlm.nih.gov/books/NBK11795/

Gomez-Pinilla, F. (2010, January 12). *Brain foods: the effects of nutrients on brain function.* NIH. https://pmc.ncbi.nlm.nih.gov/articles/PMC2805706/

Gregory, A. (2024, February 28). *Ultra-processed food linked to 32 harmful effects to health, review finds.* The Guardian. https://www.theguardian.com/society/2024/feb/28/ultra-processed-food-32-harmful-effects-health-review

In pictures: most dangerous food additives. (2012, July 12). Forbes. https://www.forbes.com/2008/04/02/food-additives-preservatives-forbeslife-cz_ph_0402additives_slide.html

Klemm, S. (2023, January 30). *Processed foods: A closer look.* Eat Right. https://www.eatright.org/health/wellness/diet-trends/processed-foods-whats-ok-and-what-to-avoid

LeWine, H. (2024, April 3). *Foods linked to better brainpower.* Harvard Health Publishing. https://www.health.harvard.edu/healthbeat/foods-linked-to-better-brainpower

Meacham, J. (2024, January 22). *What to know about emulsifers in food and personal care products.* Healthline. https://www.healthline.com/health/food-nutrition/what-are-emulsifiers

McCulloch, M. (2023, July 3). *What is sodium benzoate? Everything you need to know.* Healthline. https://www.healthline.com/nutrition/sodium-benzoate

Mikstas, C. (2024, February 23). *Is sodium nitrate safe?* WebMD. https://www.webmd.com/diet/is-sodium-nitrate-safe

Myers, I. (2024, September 19). *EWG's dirty dozen guide to food chemicals: the top 12 to avoid.* EWG. https://www.ewg.org/consumer-guides/ewgs-dirty-dozen-guide-food-chemicals-top-12-avoid

Naidoo, U. (202, October 27). *Eating well to help manage anxiety: your questions answered.* Harvard Health Publishing. https://www.health.harvard.edu/blog/eating-well-to-help-manage-anxiety-your-questions-answered-2018031413460

Natural vs. organic: does the label matter? (2019, October 1). Rodale Institute. https://rodaleinstitute.org/blog/natural-vs-organic-does-the-label-matter/

Nieto, P. (2024, August 20). *The relationship between food emulsifiers and gut health.* Tiny Health. https://www.tinyhealth.com/blog/emulsifying-the-gut-understanding-the-effects-of-food-emulsifiers-on-microbial-health

Palm oil. (n.d.). WWF. https://www.worldwildlife.org/industries/palm-oil

Petersen, A. (n.d.). *The new science on what ultra-processed food does to your brain.* LSA Psychology. https://lsa.umich.edu/psych/news-events/all-news/faculty-news/the-new-science-on-what-ultra-processed-food-does-to-your-brain.html

Reese, J. (n.d.). *What is a growth spurt during puberty?* Johns Hopkins Medicine. https://www.hopkinsmedicine.org/health/wellness-and-prevention/what-is-a-growth-spurt-during-puberty

Seitz, A. (2024, September 10). *Is maltodextrin bad for me?* Healthline. https://www.healthline.com/health/food-nutrition/is-maltodextrin-bad-for-me#what-is-maltodextrin

Sissons, B. (2023, December 22). *Is aspartame safe, and what are its side effects and health risks?* Medical News Today. https://www.medicalnewstoday.com/articles/322266

Ultra-processed foods linked to poorer brain health. (2023, May 23). Harvard T.H. Chan. https://www.hsph.harvard.edu/news/hsph-in-the-news/ultra-processed-foods-poorer-brain-health/

Ultra-processed foods: how bad are they for your health? (n.d.). British Heart Foundation. https://www.bhf.org.uk/informationsupport/heart-matters-magazine/news/behind-the-headlines/ultra-processed-foods

Zinc: good for growth. (n.d.). Healthy Children. https://www.healthychildren.org/English/ages-stages/teen/nutrition/Pages/Zinc-Good-For-Growth.aspx

Image References

Anrita1705. (2020, July 1). *Cherries, wet, washed.* [Image]. Pixabay. https://pixabay.com/photos/cherries-wet-washed-waterdrop-5360265/

Congerdesign. (2015, May 4). *Vegetables, basket, vegetable basket.* [Image]. Pixabay. https://pixabay.com/photos/vegetables-basket-vegetable-basket-752153/

Couleur. (2016, July 27). *Berries, fruits, raspberries.* [Image]. Pixabay. https://pixabay.com/photos/berries-fruits-raspberries-1546125/

Daria-Yakovleva. (2016, December 11). *Plums, box, apricots.* [Image]. Pixabay. https://pixabay.com/photos/plums-box-apricots-fruits-1898196/

Duckleap. (2023, December 10). *Woman, self-love, love.* [Image]. Pixabay. https://pixabay.com/illustrations/woman-self-love-love-hug-8439000/

Explorerbob. (2018, March 21). *Nuts, almonds, seeds.* [Image]. Pixabay. https://pixabay.com/photos/nuts-almonds-seeds-food-batch-3248743/

Hlemut_kroiss. (2020, May 9). *Vegetable stand, vegetables, market.* [Image]. Pixabay. https://pixabay.com/photos/vegetable-stand-vegetables-market-5149444/

Hyeonju88. (2017, October 6). *Vegetables, lettuce, basket.* [Image]. Pixabay. https://pixabay.com/photos/vegetables-lettuce-basket-vegetable-2826000/

Iwaro. (2017, May 28). *Avocado, fruit, vegetarian.* [Image]. Pixabay. https://pixabay.com/photos/avocado-fruit-vegetarian-the-fruit-2351191/

Jillwellington. (2015, May 31). *Vegetables, garden, harvest.* [Image]. Pixabay. https://pixabay.com/photos/vegetables-garden-harvest-organic-790022/

Jjuntune. (2014, April 10). *Vegetables, market, produce.* [Image]. Pixabay. https://pixabay.com/photos/vegetables-market-produce-food-317497/

Luiza_83. (2021, August 1). *Pickled, cucumbers, vegetable.* [Image]. Pixabay. https://pixabay.com/photos/pickled-cucumbers-vegetable-leaves-6506913/

Marcmanhart. (2017, February 16). *Cartography, map, treasure map.* [Image]. Pixabay. https://pixabay.com/vectors/cartography-map-treasure-map-2074079/

Medienservice. (2017, September 8). *Vegetables, market hall, palma.* [Image]. Pixabay. https://pixabay.com/photos/vegetables-market-hall-palma-2732589/

Mohamed_hassan. (2024, June 25). *Unbalanced, uncertainty, heart.* [Image]. Pixabay. https://pixabay.com/vectors/unbalanced-uncertainty-heart-brain-8850050/

Nadinheli22. (2017, June 8). *Supermarket, vegetables, food.* [Image]. Pixabay. https://pixabay.com/photos/supermarket-vegetables-food-shop-2384476/

Pabitrakaity. (2021, June 28). *Ads, digital marketing, advertisements.* [Image]. Pixabay. https://pixabay.com/illustrations/ads-digital-marketing-advertisements-6370790/

Roszie. (2022, October 18). *Woman, mood, mental health.* [Image]. Pixabay. https://pixabay.com/illustrations/woman-mood-mental-health-psychology-7529904/

Snowday83. (2019, July 11). *Cherry tomato, tomato, fruit.* [Image]. Pixabay. https://pixabay.com/photos/cherry-tomato-tomato-fruit-dessert-4330441/

Sponchia. (2017, October 8). *Meal, salad, cucumbers.* [Image]. Pixabay. https://pixabay.com/photos/meal-salad-cucumbers-food-leaves-2834549/